GAVIN
YOUNG

SOMETHING OF SAMOA

D1324532

PENGUIN BOOKS

PENGUIN BOOKS

Published by the Penguin Group. Penguin Books Ltd, 27 Wrights Lane, London
W8 5TZ, England. Penguin Books USA Inc., 375 Hudson Street, New York,
New York 10014, USA. Penguin Books Australia Ltd, Ringwood, Victoria, Australia.
Penguin Books Canada Ltd, 10 Alcorn Avenue, Toronto, Ontario, Canada M4V 3B2.
Penguin Books (NZ) Ltd, 182 – 190 Wairau Road, Auckland 10, New Zealand · Penguin
Books Ltd, Registered Offices: Harmondsworth, Middlesex, England · These
extracts are from *Slow Boats Home* by Gavin Young, first published by Hutchinson
& Co. (Publishers) Ltd, 1985. Published in Penguin Books 1986. This edition published 1996. Copyright © Gavin Young, 1985, 1996. All rights reserved · The moral
right of the author has been asserted · Typeset by Rowland Phototypesetting Ltd,
Bury St Edmunds, Suffolk. Printed in England by Clays Ltd, St Ives plc · Except
in the United States of America, this book is sold subject to the condition that it
shall not, by way of trade or otherwise, be lent, re-sold, hired out, or otherwise
circulated without the publisher's prior consent in any form of binding or cover other
than that in which it is published and without a similar condition including this
condition being imposed on the subsequent purchaser · 10 9 8 7 6 5 4 3 2 1

A land
In which it seemed always afternoon.

ALFRED, LORD TENNYSON: '*The Lotos-Eaters*'

Henry Betham, the shipping manager of Burns Philp in Apia, said, 'The *Pacific Islander*. Oh, yes. She's due in here in a week or so. Let's see – she's got a Japanese captain now.'

The *Pacific Islander* was the Swire container ship I had looked up in Suva. I hoped she would get me to Tahiti. Was there a new policy at Swire's China Navigation Company to employ Japanese officers – something to do with placating Nippon? It seemed unlikely.

'I don't think that can be right,' I said.

Henry, a large friendly man, checked his files again. 'No, sorry. It's Captain Carter now. It *was* Captain Ralph Kennet.'

'I know Ralph Kennet.' A couple of years before I had sailed with him from Manila to Hong Kong on another Swire vessel, the *Hupeh*.

Betham smiled. 'Well, you've got a week or so before Captain Carter gets here.' Time enough to pay my respects to R.L.S. and see something of Samoa, too.

I walked up the few steps into a two-storey white wooden

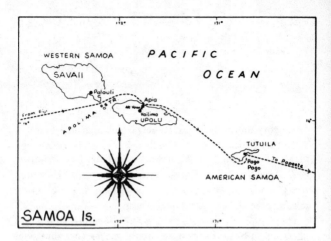

building that seemed the perfect entrance to a Samoan hotel, and found a large Samoan lady behind a counter.

'Aggie Grey?' I asked, and she shook with throaty laughter as if she had never heard anything so funny.

'Not Aggie. I'm Annie,' she said. 'Call me Big Annie, dear.' She had a room for me – 'Of course, dear' – in the garden.

Aggie Grey's Hotel stood a few hundred yards from the wharf, ideally situated with a wide view over the little bay of Apia – a famous hotel, Michael Scott had told me, owned by a handsome South Seas 'personality'. Some people thought Aggie Grey was the original of the character James Michener called Bloody Mary in the Rodgers and Hammerstein musical

South Pacific. It seemed she was in New Zealand. Her son, Alan, and his wife were in charge.

There was a book about Aggie Grey on sale in the lobby and I took a copy to my room. It told the story, the blurb said, of 'how Aggie rose to fame from selling hamburgers at her rollicking waterfront club to owning a mighty tourist complex in the South Seas'.

A mighty tourist complex? When I took a stroll I found a pleasant tangled garden and thatched-roofed guest rooms: no mighty tourist complex at all. In an open-sided bar a few tourists quietly sat over beer, and presently the sound of singing led me to a beehive-shaped thatched building where a group of young men and women in lava-lavas were rehearsing native dances, stamping and chanting with flowers in their hair.

My first Samoans were quite different from the Solomon Islanders or Fijians – no one here had a busby like Colson's, or a Papuan gargoyle face. These Polynesians had straight hair, black or dark brown, skins that were fair and faces that were almost Malaysian.

Somerset Maugham, Stevenson and Rupert Brooke had all extolled the glory of the Samoans, sometimes in such extravagant terms that one suspected poetic exaggeration. 'God's best, his sweetest work,' Stevenson had written. And now, watching these unselfconscious dancers, I knew there had been no exaggeration at all.

Aggie Grey's Hotel commanded one end of Apia's horseshoe bay, while Burns Philp's emporium and office, with Henry   3

Betham in it, stood at the other end. In between were stores, a church or two with off-white towers, a bank, and a modest complex of wooden verandahs which, a sign said, housed government offices, including the office of the Prime Minister. There can hardly be a more self-effacing Prime Minister's office in the world. Modern Apia, it was evident, had mercifully escaped the ravages of 'progressive' architects, and was still a small town. I had no difficulty in imagining the little trading station Stevenson saw in 1889 when he disembarked from his schooner, the *Equator*, and took his first brisk exploratory ramble, looking, one of Apia's merchants said later, 'like a lascar out of employment'. The emaciated writer and his family – possibly because his stepson, Lloyd Osborne, chose to wear earrings and dark glasses and carry a ukelele – were taken by the chief Anglican missionary for a troupe of scallywag vaudevillians from San Francisco. Who else, he wondered, could they be?

Stevenson's house at Vailima was still standing and his grave was now a place of pilgrimage, so it took an effort to remember that when he came here no one in this Pacific backwater had heard of Robert Louis Stevenson. Who among the German, American and British traders and plantation managers had opened any book other than a ledger or a shipping timetable? Anyway, it was the Samoans who gave him the name Tusitala, the Teller of Tales. Now he was a tourist attraction. Exploring beyond the centre of the town, I found a looming block of masonry built in the sixties or seventies with a sign which said it was the Tusitala Hotel, and its bar stocked Vailima beer.

4

In Aggie Grey's breakfast room next morning the young Samoan dancers of the day before had become smiling servants, but there were few customers. A Samoan and his jolly wife (between them they must have weighed a ton) bolted papayas and eggs and bacon and beamed around them. A sallow young white man in stained shorts blocked conversation from a pallid girl with two unvarying replies – 'No way' or 'Not likely' – while he gave an American student hints on how to travel round Samoa cadging off the natives. 'Just leave quick when they begin to look less hospitable,' he said with a snigger.

I consulted Big Annie, bought a map and a Samoan dictionary, hired a car from a European garage and headed east in it along the shore.

After two or three miles I pulled up by the roadside with a thumping heart. Of course, I had expected the magnificent, violent blue of the Pacific, beaches of pure white sand and graceful colonnades of tow-headed palm trees – all that was a common natural combination in the South Seas. Yet here it was only part of a much greater beauty.

Beehive houses, somnolent under their sun-baked thatch and raised on platforms of stones, appeared to float in a sea of brilliant foliage, their mat walls rolled up now to catch the sea breeze so that whole families were visible, sitting cross-legged, chatting and smoking, or gazing silently across the lagoon at the white tumble of foam on the reefs. Barefoot men, elegant from waist to calf in bright-coloured lava-lavas that no Paris fashion designer could improve on, and women with parasols and flower-patterned skirts, strolled on the road's edge with

5

the upright yet languorous grace that only people who walk barefoot can achieve. Village after roadside village basked serenely in the sunlight behind glistening screens of breadfruit, papaya and banana trees, frangipani, hibiscus and hedges of flowers whose names I do not know. On my map I read their soft, lilting names – Lauli'i, Salelesi, Vailele, Lufilufi. I moved on. Soon, a bumpy red-dust track swung inland, and I slowly climbed into a different world of scrub and upland trees. Villages and resplendent flowers disappeared, the sea was only visible in snatches from sharp turns along the way, and wisps of mist like an old man's beard rose from slopes of green mountains that looked two thousand feet high.

I had bumped along for perhaps an hour when I saw a house by the track. There had already been a few houses along the way, but they had been set well back, half hidden in the bush. This particular shaggy little roof lay near the road from which an apron of coral chips and flowering bushes ran up to it. A chestnut horse was hobbled by the doorposts. Behind the thatch, blue smoke rose from an open fire. I had slowed down and somebody waved. I stopped and got out of the car and a teenage girl in a lava-lava with a flower in her hair ran out of the house towards me, framed by the flowers and clouds of tiny blue butterflies.

'*Talofa*,' she said, smiling, and then unexpectedly in English, 'Will you have some food?' Her large eyes tilted up from a small, slightly flattened nose. 'My name is Emma,' she added as two women, one of them grey-haired, the other old enough to be Emma's mother, ducked out of the house, followed by a boy of eleven or twelve. A larger boy, perhaps seventeen, evidently Emma's brother, came towards the car from the bushes. 'This,' Emma patted the smaller of the two boys on the head, 'is Isaia. This is Manino.' She pointed to her mother.

The bigger boy patted his own bare chest. 'Fili,' he said. Within a minute I had been conscripted into Tolu's boisterous family.

The simplicity of the house on the empty track and Emma's wave among the flowers were the reasons for my coming to Tolu's house and my 'adoption' into his family. Not that I knew Tolu at that moment. Now I was answering five excited voices at once. 'Where are you going?'

'Just to the end of the island,' I said.

'We show you. Come!'

I hardly had time to get the doors open before Emma, Fili and Isaia dived into the car.

I had wanted to meet Samoans – well, here they were.

The eastern beaches of Samoa are everybody's dream of the *Blue Lagoon*. The one my new friends preferred looked across its inevitable reef to a green pimple in the sea, a miniature Treasure Island, it seemed, where with Captain Flint's map and a bucket and spade you could find pieces of eight in a dead man's chest. Instead, I sat quietly with Emma on sand like castor sugar while the boys splashed and screamed in turquoise water so curiously bright it looked as if it was lit artificially from below. On the way, we had discovered a family friend, Amosa, clinging halfway up an eighty-foot palm tree; his athletic descent in response to Fili's call was so immediate that he might have been waiting to join us all his life. He and Fili were in the water in a flash of limbs.

'Fili . . . ooo!'

'Amo-o-o-sa!'

Their shouts were like seabirds soaring from the lagoon or Ben Gunn's demented yodelling from the island opposite. While they played I talked of prosaic things to Emma. 'You go to school?'

Yes, she went to Lufilufi school, she said. And she was nineteen years old.

'You have a boyfriend in Lufilufi?'

'Oh, yes.' She smiled, not at all minding the question.

'You marry soon?'

She laughed. 'Oh, no.' She preferred to go to New Zealand, find work there and send money home.

'Why not work here?' Perhaps teaching English. Her English was quite good enough.

'Oh . . .'

Opposite us, the frigate-sized outcrop of Treasure Island waved its topknot of palms. Terns sideslipped in the breeze on wings that flashed like fragments of white porcelain.

'I like to see New Zealand,' said Emma. 'Then I can send money to my father. For his plantation.'

Tolu, the head of my new family, came home just before sunset and was astonished to see me. He was of medium height, stocky, with a fair paunch and a navel like the boss on a bronze breastplate. He carried a bush knife in his large and calloused hands; he had been working in his gardens, he said. The bones of his face showed that it had once been square, but a strong jaw had now become heavy and round. For about two inches above the waist of his lava-lava his skin seemed to be covered with terrible bruises, but on a closer look I saw that the 'bruises' were an elaborate tattoo encircling his body like a corset. He was pleased at my interest and drew up the hem of his lava-lava to show me how the tattoo extended round his thighs and down to his knees. The complicated dark blue patterns were densely, and no doubt painfully, pricked into his skin.

Tolu was proud of his tattoo: it conveyed noble status. '*Matei*,' he explained, pointing to himself: 'Chief.' The *South Pacific Handbook* had told me that Samoan society is based on its ten thousand chiefs, the guardians of the *fa'a Samoa*, the Samoan way of life, who elect the forty-five-member National Assembly of Chiefs in Apia. Chiefs control local affairs through the islands' village councils. Tattooing was part of *fa'a Samoa* but unfortunately it was dying out, Tolu said. I asked Fili why he was not tattooed, offering to pay for one for him, but he made a face and shook his head.

'Fili scared,' said Emma to tease him. 'Hurt too much.'

It was not easy to explain to them exactly what I was up to, but with the help of my Samoan dictionary and Emma I managed at last to convey what had brought me here and how soon I had to leave, indicating sea by holding a forearm and hand parallel to the ground and undulating it. In return I learned that Tolu, though not rich (the little house told me that), owned 9 land down the long, steep hillside out of sight of his original village by the sea. He and Fili worked a plantation of three thousand taro plants, yams, papayas, sugar, bananas and a good many coconut palms. They had cows, too, and chickens, a dog and the one chestnut horse, which was the family's sole means of transport. Nobody in Western Samoa starved: nearly all Samoans owned a 'plantation' of some size, even if some owned it indirectly through their membership of an extended family. But they had to work it. You could not let plantations go.

We sat cross-legged on woven mats, leaning against the pillars supporting the lozenge-shaped roof of sugar leaves and palm fronds. The walls consisted of adjustable panels made from woven coconut leaves, that were hoisted up and down like homespun Venetian blinds. The panels were rolled up when it was fine, so everyone and everything in the house was visible to passers-by. Not that there was much to see: a few large trunks; a plain wooden dresser full of cups, teapots and metal dishes; a deep wooden chest stuffed with schoolbooks, the family Bible, assorted clothes. Newly washed lava-lavas hung over poles in the ceiling. Meals were cooked under a separate roof behind the main house. Most dishes, I noticed, were wrapped in leaves and baked on hot stones.

After dark, when dinner was ready, Manino, with Emma and two smaller daughters, Ruta and Ala, brought in bowls of baked fish and taro spread with coconut cream and laid them on banana leaf 'plates'. Tolu murmured a prayer in Samoan, while Fili and Amosa made faces at me – I took this to mean we were now all friends together – and then we dug into the food with our fingers. The taro – a fibrous root vegetable about the size of a pineapple and the Samoan equivalent of bread – was cut into round slices as chewable as a rich fruitcake but with a dull, neutral taste; it was better dipped into coconut cream and sucked like a lollipop. Tolu sucked each fishbone, too, loudly and with great care, before spitting it into his hand. Any food that spilled on to the mat-covered floor was cleaned up by two furtive cats that cleverly dodged slaps from Fili and ignored Isaia's whispers of 'Pussi, pussi.'

A humid heat lingered long after the sun had gone down in a blaze behind the forest and the last fruit bats had flapped heavily home. Flying insects were the problem. Throughout the meal they did their best to disrupt us. Smack! Smack! The family slapped arms, legs and bare torsos as swarms of indefatigable mosquitoes sniped at us like highly trained hit-and-run guerrillas. Struggling with fishbones, I could see these 'winged blood-drops' placidly grazing on my vulnerable arms and feet and feel needlelike bites on my neck and forehead. They crawled boldly into one's ears. It was difficult to eat and just as hard to relax later; the teasing, remorseless whine continued long after the dishes had been cleared away and even after the side walls of the house had been lowered for the night. Fili covered my feet with a spare lava-lava and Isaia squatted down by me and began flapping a leaf-shaped woven fan round my ears, but I wondered how I was going to sleep. Stevenson hardly mentions the mosquitoes at Vailima, yet they must have been a nightmare for a writer with no insecticide and little or no window netting. Had he forgotten this little bit of hell in paradise? With the moon, a cool breeze came like a blessing and Tolu yawned, evidently a signal for Fili and Amosa to drag up mattresses and pillows. 'You sleep here,' Fili said, patting a mattress by his own. This was luxury. I had expected to sleep on the bare mat. More than that, there were to be some anti-mosquito measures: Amosa unfurled three huge nets over the mattresses and soon, at long last, the infernal whining died away and I saw some possibility of sleep. I heard the muffled shifting of springs: Isaia had begged to be allowed to guard the car and had curled up in the back seat. Then Amosa went home, murmuring '*Tofa*.'

''*Fa*, Amosa.'

When Tolu lowered the flame in the pressure lamp, the mosquito nets seemed to swell in the dark and fill the little house like three white phantoms. In the silence, like a hundred sewing machines, the cicada chorus began in the undergrowth outside. The chestnut horse, tethered to a banana tree, blew now and again and stamped a hoof. A dog barked on the hillside.

'Gavin stay one week,' Emma called in the darkness.

'Gavin stay one year,' Fili said.

'Gavin stay,' Tolu gruffly told his family, cutting the talking short.

I watched moonlight seeping through the wall blinds and listened to the night. The breeze rapped the bamboos; a nightjar chuckled behind the house.

'I stay,' I said, giving in to the Samoan night. To them all.

The early morning was as cool and fresh as if Samoa had been created that very sunrise. Dew gleamed on each banana leaf, on every blade of grass, on every hibiscus blossom and gardenia. The smoke of Manino's fire hung motionless round her kitchen like a blue horizontal screen, giving out the smell of roasting cocoa beans. I had roused Isaia from the car by tickling his feet, and he held a bowl of water as I cleaned my teeth with a clump of sugarcane. Fili hacked firewood and soon Amosa strolled up, his nose deep in the petals of a gardenia.

'*Talofa*, Gavin.'

'*Talofa*, Amosa.'

With Fili and Amosa, I pushed through thick bush to a deep, stony cleft where water ran so cold that the first plunge took my breath away. The two Samoans, apparently unaffected, splashed and laughed, warmed by a halo of sun. Stevenson had written of such scenes. In his time, not so very long ago, war drums had sounded on this very hillside, and warriors had raced home through these trees from battles, waving the heads of their enemies and crying excitedly to their chiefs, 'I have taken a man!' It was easy to imagine those days of severed heads in this hidden untouched place where the great trees, scores of years old, trailed feathery creepers like hairy arms. Amosa and

Fili conversed in high-pitched cries like bird calls, and their singing was falsetto, too. On our way back to Tolu and with the house in sight, I was suddenly alone – they had taken off like a brace of excited snipe, racing through a field of waist-high taro plants, zigzagging through the upturned, heart-shaped leaves which swayed out of their path like an army of green, flat-faced extraterrestrial beings taken by surprise. Amosa, with his gardenia in his hand, his yellow lava-lava, his brown limbs and his streaming hair, might easily have been some wood demon spirit of the place celebrating another fine day.

Samoan superstition peoples the island with spirits. Belief in ghosts runs in the blood, and where a people speak of ghosts the phantoms tend to respond. Known in Samoa as *aitus*, they dwell in every tree and stream, as *jinns* live in the hills and groves of Arabia. According to local tradition Apia is a sort of spirits' transit camp, a seaside springboard from which they launch themselves into *Pulotu*, the Other World. Stevenson wrote that he had an *aitu* for a neighbour at Vailima – 'It is a lady, *Aitu fafine*: she lives in the mountainside; her presence is heralded by the sound of a gust of wind, a sound very common in the high woods; when she catches you, I do not know what happens; but in practice she is avoided, so I suppose she does more than pass the time of day.'

Little Isaia shared Amosa's puckish quality. He frisked about in as sprightly a way as any child I have ever met.

I tapped his nose very gently with my finger. 'You . . . are . . . an . . . *aitu*!'

'*Aitu!*' – delighted, Isaia ran hysterically around Tolu's banana patch, scattering the chickens.

'*Aitu!*' Emma screamed.

I saw Manino laughing behind her cooking pots, and Tolu, too, called, 'Isaia is *aitu*.'

Across the commotion, Amosa smiled his wood demon's smile at me over his gardenia and closed one slanting, green eye in what might have been a conspiratorial wink.

Whack! A huge, middle-aged *matai* in a black-and-yellow lava-lava swung his three-sided bat at the ball hurled directly at his stomach and smacked it over the copra trees towards the sea. Gathering up their lava-lavas, three fielders rushed headlong to retrieve it from a tangle of morning glories. The most head-long of them, I saw, was Tolu.

His village was playing cricket against a neighbouring village.

Whack! The next ball soared inland and for a long time a number of boys feverishly searched the undergrowth. Ten minutes went by . . . fifteen. No one showed impatience. You could tell from the crowds of onlookers that *kirikiti*'s import-ance to Samoans easily transcended long hold-ups like this. The hold-ups, I soon saw, were frequent because Samoan cricket is a more straightforward game than its British model. You cannot be out leg before wicket because no one wears pads and so fancy play becomes physically dangerous. No one can be bothered to block a ball, and because batsmen are warriors at play, blocking is not very highly considered. Manhood demands a virile swing of the bat – of the warclub, really – and Samoans usually hit the ball. Nine times out of ten it flies high over the short jungle boundaries – it is made of light rubber – and the long search begins. To be out, you must be caught or bowled.

There are frequent casualties. Tolu had explained that the suppurating sore I had noticed on his leg was a cricket injury. Chasing a ball from pitch to beach he had stumbled into coral, a dangerous thing to be cut by because it leaves poisoned gashes. But worse wounds than that can be sustained in Samoan cricket. Teams of twenty or twenty-five hot-blooded players have been known to turn village rivalry into real war, and now and again when that happens a bad sportsman, or umpire, is sometimes chased and clubbed to death.

On this occasion propriety reigned. Sportsmanlike handclaps rose from groups of figures smoking in the shade of breadfruit trees, and spectators perched like bright birds halfway up the trunks of coconut palms cheered and called encouragement to the batsmen who one after the other strode fiercely to the wicket, clutching their bats like semi-naked warriors advancing to lop off a few heads.

Amosa and Fili were not playing at warriors or sportsmen. They sat in long grass singing in falsetto to a small guitar. 'We go,' said Fili when it was quite dark.

Soon clouds hid the rising moon and spits of rain splashed the windscreen. The headlights wavered along the long, steep forest track, illuminating boys carrying baskets of coconuts, women holding umbrellas over small children, half-naked men on dripping horses. The wet, bare calves, shoulders, chests made shining patterns of brown and gold. After a while there were no more human beings and then suddenly the lane opened out. The grey tower of a church and thatched houses loomed as unreal as an exotic film set. There were figures on the roadside, shaking fists, waving. Young men were shouting, running frantically from the deep shadow of trees and bushes. They looked demented. Had there been a terrible accident?

I began to slow down. The last thing I expected was that Fili and Amosa would go berserk. But I felt Fili pummelling my shoulders from the back seat, and heard Amosa beside me yelling – 'Go, go, go! Stop no! Stop – no!'

Figures gibbered and gesticulated.

'Go to home!' Fili shouted. 'Bad, bad!'

Battered and half deafened, I accelerated recklessly, wrenching the car away from what looked like a mob of madmen throwing themselves at our headlights. I shall never know how I did not run down at least two of them. Was it a hold-up? Wild, indecipherable words were lost in the night. I remember close-up, split-second images of open, twisted mouths, flying hair, furious eyes at the window. Worse – dark, solid objects flew across my vision towards the by now swiftly moving car.

'Fili – what . . . ?' I swerved to miss the trunk of a perfume tree.

'Go, go!' Fili was breathless with passion.

After a minute I slowed down. 'Now then,' I said, and now it was explained.

'Very bad boys and girls. Come from New Zealand. Too

much beer, too much –' Fili mimed a man smoking and his finger drew circles round his temple. Drugs.

'*Kkhhhh! Kkkhhhh!*' Amosa's exclamation conveyed the strongest disgust. It was an odd, harsh sound, half gargle, half growl, like a file against a knot of wood.

So that was it. We had run into a coven of boozy and very violent Samoan layabouts – typical, according to Fili and Amosa, of most young emigrants to New Zealand. There they had acquired a taste for liquor, drugs and fighting. Girls as well as boys. Lost souls. A serious menace to an innocent, church-going population. As a Methodist, Fili said sententiously, he thoroughly disapproved of alcohol. It made Samoans behave like animals. Those solid flying objects had been bottles. For drunken fun, they would have damaged the car, and beaten us up. Kkkhhh!

'What about the police?'

Fili said, impatiently, 'Police only in Apia.'

'Girls very bad,' Amosa said. 'Drink beer then make –' Gestures told me what they did.

'With you, Amosa?'

'No, no! Me-tho-dist!' he cried righteously.

Fili interrupted. 'Amosa like *fu-fu* with girl.'

'*Fu-fu?*'

More vivid gestures assailed my eyes in the rear-view mirror. *Fu-fu* evidently meant what used to be known as heavy petting.

'Fili like *moetotolo*,' Amosa said in one-upmanlike tones.

'*Moeto –?*' I dodged a troop of piglets that charged across the track behind a sow big enough to have overturned the car.

But the panic was over. Fili and Amosa soon settled down again and we drove home to the sound of falsetto Samoan singing. The mosquitoes were as bad as ever, but Manino had cooked green pigeons and spotted crabs for dinner.

The Methodist minister, a Samoan in his mid-thirties who had spent some years in Australia, was Tolu's friend and neighbour. His bungalow and church stood by the track a few hundred yards away.

'*Moetotolo* – so you've heard of that.' The minister seemed amused. '"Night-creeping", in other words. Very common in Samoa.'

His wife gave a polite little laugh over her teacups.

The aim of *moetotolo* was for a young man to steal a girl's virginity as she slept in her parents' house. I had seen how a Samoan family slept side by side, sharing mats and mosquito nets, and I found it difficult to imagine how on earth Amosa, say, could deflower poor Emma and against her will without raising the household within half a minute. What contortions would do the trick? Surely it was impossible. And the boy would be courting serious physical harm – if the girl's father and brothers woke up, they might beat him to death.

'Of course,' the minister said, seriously, 'it is a *manual* deflowering. Not a . . . full-scale . . .'

'And the object?' I asked. 'Just the thrill?'

Tolu said, the minister translating, 'The only motive is to force the girl to marry him. From shame . . . You see, if the boy steals her virginity,' the minister went on, 'he shames her 19 deeply. Shame is a strong element in a girl's make-up, so he will threaten to tell the village unless she agrees to marry him.'

The minister's handsome wife lay now on her stomach on a mat on the floor, her arms and chin resting on a bolster. She said, 'It happened near here only the other day.'

The minister said, 'Yes. This boy comes creeping in the night to the girl sleeping among her family. He makes *moetotolo*. But he is clumsy. The girl jumps up and shouts to her father. The father wakes up and this boy is all tangled up in the mosquito net. The boy runs too late. The father catches him and beats him very badly. Then the father complains to the *matais'* village council and they fine the father of the boy – pigs, a hundred taros, some fine woven mats: a heavy fine in these parts.'

The minister's Bible lay on a chair and, to see what Samoan looked like, I turned to the first words of all: '*Na faia e le Atua ma le lalolagi i le amataga . . .*' ('In the beginning God created the world . . .'). The Gospels here were according to Mataio, Mareko, Luka and Ioane. Amosa, I discovered, was Samoan for Moses.

'Drink,' said the minister. 'Drugs. That's the serious problem. Growing fast, I'm afraid. *Kava*, the traditional root drink we make here, that's all right – that calms you and sends you to sleep; nobody fights on *kava*. But the grog that comes from Apia or Pago-Pago in American Samoa – whisky, gin, vodka – and the drugs brought in by hippies and tourists – marijuana, cocaine, heroin from Auckland or Sydney – that's another matter. The chiefs here ban liquor in their villages but, all the same, young Samoan men and women who learnt to drink in New Zealand do it secretly in the bush at night, as you saw. In New Zealand they learn to reject *fa'a Samoa* – the Samoan way of life. That's what it amounts to.' He smiled. 'I don't mind telling you, I was a whisky and drugs man myself when I was studying in Australia. Oh yes, I was. Of course, that's all over now. But it shows I know what I'm talking about.'

Outside, Samoan matrons, demure in white blouses and ankle-length skirts, were coming down the path, leading their children to the minister's Bible class.

'What is happening to the essence and charm of Samoan traditional culture? We cherish it so much – oh, so much. Why should our people be forced to change by Western progress?'

The minister himself was a good example of Samoan charm and vitality. But a few days previously I had driven to visit a different sort of pastor on the south coast who had recently married Tolu's sister – an old man, a Congregationalist with a tight, lipless mouth. The pastor had held an evening prayer meeting in his low, barnlike house by the sea. About ten rows of his parishioners squatted before him under the corrugated iron roof in the dim oil light, listening to interminable prayers and verses of the Bible intoned in a dry voice that seemed quite devoid of compassion – or even of life. The mosquitoes there had made the night unbearable, and in the morning their bites had puffed up my eyes like a boxer's. At breakfast he had eyed his plump wife as she tucked into her taro and murmured sourly, 'Greed is *not* one of the virtues.'

'We are not accustomed to visitors like you. We used to get 21 many visitors!' the old man said before I left to return to Tolu's. 'Americans. Not so many now.'

'Why not now?'

He gave me a hard glance. 'I always asked them for their passports when they wanted to stay. Well, the Prime Minister had warned us that foreigners, Americans mostly, were bringing drugs into Samoa.'

'How did they take that? You asking them for their passports, I mean.'

He cackled with satisfaction. 'They'd go away and not come back. Not many come now.'

Would he ask me for my passport? I waited but he didn't.

Instead, he leaned towards me. 'Tell me, Mr Gavin – if modern development means the dehumanization of societies, what is the use of it? No one starves here. These islands – their plantations – could support five or six times the present population. Instead, young people neglect their plantations. They drift to towns, buy beer, see imported X-rated movies, lounge about – go, I suppose one might say, to hell. We Samoans have a paradise here. Do you agree?'

'Yes, I do,' I said. He might not be one of the most lovable citizens of this paradise, but I agreed with him that it was one. Many Samoans, I thought, must be haunted by the image of Apia destroyed by concrete and neon, every thatched house showing reruns of *Dallas*.

To Tolu's neighbour, the young minister, I said now, 'Stick to *fa'a Samoa* like grim death.'

22   Animated women followed by little girls with white bows in

their hair were coming in. There was much laughter and spirited chat.

He nodded. 'Travel doesn't always just broaden the mind, does it?' He got up and began to greet his ebullient parishioners. Over his shoulder he called, 'As far as we are concerned, it can destroy it, too.'

After a few days with Tolu I drove to Apia. The excursion ended dramatically. My notebook records:

Two unprepossessing Samoans thumb lift. They wear jeans and T-shirts, their hair is wild, their chins stubbly, their eyes red. One has two missing front teeth. Will I take them to Apia? 'All right, get in.' After five minutes on the road, one of them says abruptly, 'Turn off here. We'll go to such-and-such-a-village.'

Dutifully, I turn off. We drive for some time on a road that climbs into the bush; there is no sign of a village or even a house. It is disturbing. Am I being hijacked? I have an uneasy feeling that they are communicating with each other secretly, with winks and glances.

I say, 'Well, where is the village?'

They talk in Samoan together.

The one with missing teeth gives a sickly snigger – 'Oh, we'll go to Apia instead.' No explanation.

Odd – and sinister. I turn the car with relief. At Apia market they get out. A shaggy head pokes through the window. 'Will you take us back in half an hour?' Vodka wafts about me. I tell them I am staying the night in Apia.

'Oh,' and they shrug and walk off.

But that was not the end. The same evening, in Aggie Grey's bar, a waiter says a friend of mine is outside. A friend?

'Says he your *best* friend.'

It was one of the two hitchhikers, swaying, his eyes blood-red. He looked terrible, clearly drugged but reeking of liquor too. He also looked violent. The two middle-aged Samoan businessmen I had been with in the bar came out and talked soothingly to him. Money, he said, or a drink. We gave him money and luckily he staggered away into the night. One of the businessmen said, 'Never give a lift to such people. Did you see? On his forearm he has a tattoo – "Deported from New Zealand".'

'Don't say the New Zealand Government tattoos deportees!' It seemed barbaric.

'Oh, he probably tattooed it himself. Some of these Samoan druggies are proud to have been deported from, or even jailed in, New Zealand. They think it gives them status among Samoans here who haven't been abroad. Did you know Auckland has a bigger Samoan population than any city in the world? Very many unemployed.'

His friend said, 'Drunkenness, muggings, killings, too.'

'Yes, a lot of that.'

In the morning, the singing, dancing waiters and waitresses were rehearsing in the same beehive house. I watch them, hypnotized again by so much beauty and enthusiasm. The songs were conducted by the wife of Aggie Grey's son Alan, and later she gave me the words of one of the songs, translated (very roughly) from Samoan:

Samoan teenagers ready to go abroad,
Remember Samoa's name and be safe and free.

So many problems come up over there
And a Samoan is blamed for causing the lot.

Thirty days is your permit to stay in New Zealand,
Yet towards the end you overstayed,
Hiding and sneaking so joyfully.
When you are caught, you know it's deportation.
Why not be more careful and stay honest?

You come back so pale and white.
You've gained nothing, and you're just a fiery barrel of trouble.
Forget all about these motor cars and that la di da English.
Time is precious. Do something useful. Get to work on a banana
    plantation.

So people are so worried about the emigration problem it has
even been put to music. I told them I hoped the song would
go to the top of the Samoan charts. It is there already, they
said, smiling. I wondered: if these boys and girls go to New
Zealand, how great is the chance that they, too, will become
denimed derelicts?

The sight of a Catholic mission down the road from Aggie
Grey's stirred a happy, if flippant, memory. Clipped, unmistak-
able tones sang wickedly in my head:

The natives greeted them kindly and invited them to dine
On yams and clams and human hams and vintage coconut wine,
The taste of which was filthy, but the after-effects divine . . .

Pace Noël Coward's Uncle Harry, there had been severed heads
26 in Samoa but no edible human hams. Still, the local *kava* I had

tried with Tolu's friends, though bitter, had a pleasant calming effect.

> They didn't brandish knives at him, they were really awfully sweet,
> They made concerted dives at him and offered him things to eat,
> But when they threw their wives at him he had to admit defeat.
> Uncle Harry's not a missionary now – he's on the island –
> But he's certainly not a missionary now.

I had never met a South Seas missionary and I need hardly say that the venerable Catholic priest I called on was quite unlike poor lapsed Uncle Harry. He was good to talk to because he loved Samoa, speaking the language, knowing the islands as he knew his Bible. He was a humorous Irishman, had been here many years. Indeed, he was not really a missionary at all. Catholics had long ago given up chasing converts. Why convert the converted? By now, he said, Samoans are ninety per cent Christian, so what was the point in Christian proselytizing? That would be to steal from friends – the Methodists, Congregationalists, Seventh Day Adventists, the Assembly of God people, and all the rest. Samoans had not been pagan for a hundred years or more. 'Samoa is founded on God', after all, is the national motto. 'We are not against lava-lavas,' he said, 'or tattooing or *kava* ceremonies, or singing or dancing. Let me put our attitude like this: we are not against the Samoan way of life – on the contrary we, so to speak, baptize the *fa'a Samoa*. D'ye see? . . . Only the Mormons are recruiting,' he continued sadly. 'Strenuously recruiting, I'd say.' They seemed to him to go about like the United States Marine Corps, spending enormous sums on advertising – literally millions, perhaps billions, of dollars – across the world. I forget now if it was this quiet Catholic or Tolu's Methodist neighbour who gave it as his opinion that the Mormons were sometimes not above bribing chiefs to join them. If you could net a chief you could land the whole family. Of course, this may have been sour grapes.

The old Irishman didn't look sour. He said, 'They are buying land all over. They are building modern, American churches imported from Utah. They are building a multimillion-dollar temple here in Apia. You see, the Mormon Church is a great worldwide business, into mines, shipping, supermarkets.' He made it sound a bit like Goldfinger, General Motors and Billy Graham rolled into one.

I went to have a look at the great temple.

The Mormon headquarters in Apia certainly looked as if it meant big business. In this sleepy town, on this sleepy green island, it was quite shockingly incongruous, though it would probably attract little notice in Hawaii. Its complex of neat, air-conditioned buildings reminded me of a newly built American Army headquarters in Vietnam. Americans with short hair, in crisp white shirts, walked briskly in and out of doors marked 'Education Department' and 'Real Estate Department'. Shining pickup trucks with 'Love One Another' stickers on them stood in parking bays. It was all 'go'. I half expected to see a helicopter pad, a P X store and people exchanging military salutes.

The Irishman had been right about the new temple. It was not finished but you could see there was going to be nothing cheap about it. It resembled a combined nuclear fall-out shelter, concert hall and ultra-modern city crematorium, and it was designed to be noticed. Its soaring spire would certainly attract the awe of Samoans of one sort or another.

In a cool office an American woman sat behind a rectangular name plaque on her desk and said: 'Sure, the temple is very costly. It's made of very costly material, mostly in white and gold. Three million dollars' worth, I understand. You could check that out from our Dale Cook from Utah. He's in charge of construction.'

I gave Dale Cook a miss, but saw instead the man in charge of the Mormons in Samoa, President Carl Harris, a slim, confident, fortyish man in a white short-sleeved shirt and a striped tie. He kindly offered me a cup of coffee in his office.

'We have a duty,' he said when I asked about missionaries and proselytizing in Samoa, 'to take the Gospel to the four corners of the earth, just as our Scriptures tell us to. When we read John in *Revelations* saying that he saw an angel in the midst of heaven carrying the everlasting gospel – we take this as applying to the present time. The Mormons have a hundred and eighty-three missions around the world now, and we have a duty.'

Outside President Harris's office, Samoan youths and girls stood about in an orderly fashion in short-sleeved white shirts and black ties that gave them the goody-goody air of senior prefects at an exclusive school.

They wore identity badges, too – the boys were 'Elders', the girls 'Sisters' – like members of a convention or a military 29 mess. None of them wore flowers in their hair. I had already seen young Samoans with ties and shirts in the streets of Apia self-consciously walking in pairs. It would be unfair to describe them as zombies, but they didn't seem quite real either. They were nothing like Tolu or Fili or Amosa. Carl Harris explained this.

'We like them to walk in pairs of the *same* sex – because our Scriptures say it's better that way. A boy or girl alone might feel discouraged, but two can buoy one another up.'

He smiled ruefully, shaking his head. 'Sometimes Samoans act very young. They believe in eat, drink, be merry – and then some. That's their trouble.'

He shrugged. 'So we must be strict. No dating with the opposite sex. Rigorous study. More and more proselytizing. And, of course, self-discipline: we ask them to refrain from rugby, cricket, swimming. And there's to be no dancing, naturally.'

Questions about *fu-fu* and *moetotolo* withered under Mr Harris's steady Dr Arnold of Rugby gaze. I asked myself a question. What was the point in turning lively young Samoans into self-satisfied, buttoned-down youths from Utah?

On the wall, rows of photographs with names under them ('Elder This' and 'Sister That') stared down with the blank look you see in all passport pictures. These were the Samoan converts, now 'on mission'. President Harris saw my interest in them and said, 'Those hundred and seventy boys and girls on the wall are working in Western and American Samoa today. We have about thirty-six thousand in the two Samoas now.' A number to boast about in a population of a hundred and ninety thousand, already mostly Christian for decades. 'Of course, some have been called outside Samoa. To Los Angeles, Guam and New Zealand. And, of course, to our Mormon University in Hawaii.'

I stared at him, wondering whether separating Samoans from their islands and their *fa'a Samoa* was what God really wanted for 'His sweetest work'. The other churches on the island did not think so.

I thanked President Harris and went out into the sun, passing the boys and girls standing about outside in ties and shirts and badges, and drove back to Aggie Grey's. It was nice to see Mount Vaea's green hump in the sun and the shine on the bay. Nice, too, to be greeted at the hotel by Big Annie and one of the waiters I'd seen dancing and singing in the garden. I knew he wasn't a Mormon; he wasn't wearing a tie. He was probably a Methodist. Whatever he was, he was a real Samoan. I gave him a big smile.

I had to check on my next ship.

The *Pacific Islander* would be on time, Henry Betham said when we consulted his telex messages at Burns Philp. So I prepared to return to Tolu's for my farewells to Samoa. I bought large bags of rice, sugar and tea, corned beef, baked beans, biscuits – all the things Manino had asked for.

It was raining when I reached the house. Great silver drops ran down the flanks of the horse tethered on the coral chips at the door. Fili was chopping taro, his hair dripping, his sopping 31 lava-lava clinging to his thighs – lopping the stalks off the fat, edible roots with his long bush knife and tossing them into a coconut-frond basket like a Samoan warrior of a hundred years ago, tossing enemy heads before his chief. He greeted me with an arm thrown about my neck, shouting '*Talofa!*', and I went in to meet Tolu and the others with a wet smear of dark brown earth down one cheek.

There was to be a feast. Manino had made a dish called *palusami*, a delicious, yogurty, spinachy mess of coconut cream, onion and salt, wrapped and baked among hot stones in taro, banana and breadfruit leaves.

Soon, Amosa brought in a piglet in a woven basket. He and Fili laid the squealing brute on its back, placed a stout but slender pole across its throat and stood with both feet and their whole weight on the pole, one at each end. The pig choked to death, taking its time.

. Not that I waited. Unable to watch this public murder, I drove Manino and Isaia to the lagoon where they scoured the shore for red-lacquered crabs with yellow bellies and large spots the colour of dried blood on their backs, smaller white-bellied crabs, sea slugs, cockles (*pee-pee*), and the speckled cowries whose shells, with their varnished look and jagged mouths, are in Europe usually decorations on a mantelshelf. (I found their contents hard and rubbery, impossible to chew without making your jaw ache.)

It had stopped raining as we drove back from the sea. Pink and blue strips of sunset sky lit the horizon. The black wings of solitary flying foxes flapped home overhead. Muscular young men like the bareback cavaliers of a medieval army rode down the track, or led horses straddled with loads of coconuts.

'*Tofa*, Isaia!' they called.

''*Fa*, Ioane!'

''*Fa!* '*Fa!*'

The voices came and went in the dark now. The pressure lamps glowed in homes along the way, turning them into friendly dolls' houses.

Tolu's prayer tonight was a long one.

'*Le Atua ua matou faafetai . . .*' (Emma wrote it out for me later). '*Fesoasaoni mai i la matou mafutaga ma Gavin . . . Amene.*' 'O God, we thank you for your love . . . and help us to strengthen our fellowship with Gavin. Guide him safely to his country. This is our prayer. In Jesus' name.' There was much more, and while Tolu's deep voice rumbled on I looked surreptitiously at the others. The women buried their heads in their hands – the old woman bent double on her mat in an attitude of devotional abandon. Fili and Amosa made hideous faces. Then the meal came. Along with the shellfish and the poor piglet, now baked in hot stones, we ate mullet and pieces of a fat white squid caught by Tolu.

Afterwards it was present-time. I had bought a good Seiko watch for Fili, a smaller one for Manino and a tiny digital watch for Isaia which reduced him to tears. I gave Tolu my rubber-sealed torch, but I had three Parker pens for him, too. I had a beautiful lava-lava each for Emma and the old woman, two fine lava-lavas for Amosa, and a large bag of sweets for the little ones, Ruta and Ala. In return, the old lady presented me 33 with a fine mat she had woven and hemmed with scarlet feathers; Isaia gave me a basket; Emma a prayerbook with an inscription in ink – 'This Belongs To You, Gavin, Please Do Not Forget Me, Love Always, Emma Tolu.'

Fili was holding out an amazing piece of local art: an upturned half-coconut shell on tiny pillars, a decorative circle of cowrie shells: a model of a Samoan chief's assembly hall. How could I pack that? A letter went with it. 'To My Dearest Friend, This is my *meaalofa* [present] to you my best friend. Don't forget me, because I didn't forget you my best friend . . . I love always for you, G. Young.' Amosa knelt to hang a necklace of cowrie shells round my neck, and, on behalf of the family, Tolu took from a wooden chest a heavy Bible in Samoan, 'For you,' he said.

Later, I lay under the mosquito net, listening for the last time to the rain thrumming on the thatched roof and the wind clattering the bamboos like a witch-doctor making music on old bones. The wind reminded me of something Stevenson had said: 'I have always feared the sound of wind beyond everything. In my hell, it would always blow a gale.' But this was no gale. The night was soft and peaceful.

Something scuttled across my neck, settled there, moved slowly on my shoulder . . . a tarantula – the Speckled Band? A hot iron seemed to touch my skin, and I leaped up, shouting – 'Hey, Fili! Snake!' That roused the house. Tolu searched the mattress with the torch I'd just given him, while my neck and shoulder burned like fire. Between us we found it in the end, 34 looking down at us from the mosquito netting – a centipede, the biggest I have ever seen, three inches long. '*Atualoa*,' Emma said when it lay crushed by Tolu's foot. It was a pretty name for a centipede. 'It came to kiss goodbye.'

They laughed when I said I hoped the *atualoa* wasn't an important *aitu* in disguise.

I drove to Apia early next morning. I was in a good mood for a funeral, though the car looked fit for a wedding. Isaia and Ruta had collected hibiscus and gardenia blossoms and strewn them on the bonnet and decorated the dashboard with frangipani flowers. Emma had tied a flowering creeper a yard long to the radio aerial so that it would stream behind us when I moved off. And Amosa arrived with a flower in his ear and a bush lime as a nosegay. The car smelled like a florist's and sounded like a music parlour – Fili and Amosa sang all the way to Apia and always in falsetto. Tolu, Manino, Emma and Isaia followed us in a bus with a load of Tolu's copra. It was too messy for the car, he said.

At Aggie Grey's Fili peered at my books. 'This book? Mormon?' He held up the hotel copy of *The Book of Mormon*, in which a former occupant of the room had scribbled: 'All complete bullshit stories for small children.' From the frontispiece the Mormons' Prophet, Joseph Smith in a buff coat, looked at us with a pleasant, innocuous face. Next Amosa dug my old metal flask of whisky out of my bag.

'Medicine,' I said. 'Not for you. For me.'

'*Bad!*' he retorted, undeceived. '*Kkkhhhh!*'

They scrutinized my maps, examined my clothes, tasted my 35

toothpaste. They might have been detectives investigating a prime murder suspect.

'All right, I'm guilty,' I said. 'Come on, we go.' But it took a little longer.

The room was suddenly flooded with evangelism – the Revival Time Choir from American Samoa singing a song entitled 'Eternal Life'. Amosa was carefully combing his long hair with my comb. 'Sing along as Brother MacClellan leads us,' said a radio voice as sludgy as cold molasses, but Fili was struggling into my *Chengtu* T-shirt. I switched off the radio abruptly and wrenched the T-shirt from Fili's back. Then we went to join the others at the market. At last I was going to pay my respects to R.L.S.

When work is over Louis sat down to rest,
and sighed for a cigarette . . . At that moment Sosimo [his valet]
appeared with the tobacco. '*Quel e le potu*,' said Lou gratefully, 'How
great is the wisdom,' and was deeply touched by the quick reply,
'How great is the love!'

MRS STEVENSON: *Letters from Samoa*

The pass from the Prime Minister's Department was made out to me alone, so Tolu and his family agreed to loll about under the great trees at the foot of Mount Vaea while I looked round the house. I could see that since Vailima had become the guest house of Samoa's head of state it had been expanded; it was rather wider than the house Stevenson built in 1892 with the wood he had expensively shipped from San Francisco. Yet the original was still there, too. It was beautifully situated among the great trees, its porch half buried in flowering creepers. It was empty now; seldom used. A pale, white-haired, white-clothed figure met me on the verandah steps. 'Miki Lalogi,' it whispered its name, smiling. This was the cook and guardian I had been told to expect – half-Samoan, half-German, born here. Quite old and very friendly, he was pleased to have a visitor.

I recognized the airy verandah from old photographs in R.L.S.'s *Letters*: its white, wooden ceiling fourteen feet high, its great width. I had the two books of Stevenson letters with me – Louis' and his mother's – and I showed Miki Lalogi the photographs they had taken here and what old Mrs Stevenson had written on this house:

. . . the pleasant hours we spend grouped on the verandah whither we always betake ourselves after meals; lounging on easy chairs or squatting on mats, according to taste. The verandah is twelve foot wide, and as it goes round three sides of the house, we can always be sure of shade: I wish I could add of breeze also, but that is not so easily to be contrived.

He nodded his old white head and pointed at a sepia photograph of the verandah. 'It is the same,' he said. We could not contrive a breeze today any more than the Stevensons had. Even at nine o'clock in the morning it was warming up. Soon it would be uncomfortable. In the Great Hall there was nothing but a long table now. You had to imagine the oil lamps, the *chaises longues*, the kneeling ceramic or wooden buddhas guarding the wide staircase – and Louis Stevenson himself, long-legged, skeletal, moustachioed, nervously pacing up and down the waxed floor. And old Mrs S., looking like a thin Queen Victoria, sipping brandy and soda and nibbling ship's biscuits, scattering the crumbs, talking to Fanny, Lou's wife, who sat sombrely watching her restless husband and smoking. Where we stood now, Lou had read aloud chapters of *The Wreckers* and *Weir of Hermiston*.

On the stairs I felt sweat prickling my forehead. No wonder R.L.S. worked best at sunrise. In his bedroom, now a library, there was a framed poem by Rabindranath Tagore on one wall:

Our voyage is done
We bow to Thee, our Captain . . .

Bookcases held hundred-year-old Tauchnitz editions, published in Leipzig. *Zanoni* and *Kenelm Chillingly* by Sir Edward Bulwer Lytton, Conan Doyle's *The Stark Munro Letters* and Wilkie Collins' *No Name* and *Hide and Seek* – how many people living have read those novels? Who has heard of Rider Haggard's *Jess*, his *The Witch's Head* or his *Joan Haste*? Across two shelves were ranged the complete works of R.L.S. himself, in the Heinemann Vailima edition of 1922, and an 1898 copy of *St Ives*.

The room was quite airless, and smelled of must and dust. A dying fly lay on its back, filling the silence with its buzzing. 'There is one novelty that ought to prove a comfort,' said Mrs Stevenson again from the pages in my hand. 'The doors and windows are closed in with wire gauze, so that it is insect-proof, and I can sleep without a mosquito net. Moreover, I hope that horrid creature, the mason bee, won't be able to get into my books and spoil them.' There were no mason bees in evidence, and no wire gauze either.

The study had a sketch by Belle Strong of R.L.S. reading to his wife, from which we were distracted by an extraordinary sound from the front lawn. A most peculiar brass band was trying its best to strike up 'Colonel Bogey', but total disarray prevented struggling tubas, sousaphones and trombones from matching key for key, failing even to match oompah for 39 oompah, and half the bandsmen were collapsed in helpless laughter on the grass, rolling about among their shiny, dented instruments. One or two wore uniform jackets of an unidentifiable (and unmatching) order. Most had bare torsos, though a very few had ragged shirts. A saxophonist, flat on his back, convulsed in hysterics, looked like a pirate in green headscarf and purple lava-lava. My ghostly guide, Miki, giggled. 'Apia police band,' he whispered. 'Practice.'

From the anarchy on the lawn I could look straight up at Mount Vaea, which seemed only touching distance away. Stevenson had leaned from this louvred window the morning of the day he died, aged forty-four, of a cerebral haemorrhage; he had gazed up at the mountain almost as if he had a premonition of death. His gardener, Lafaele, standing where the big drum banged now, had seen him and waved, and Stevenson had called '*Talofa!*'

I could see a semicircular gleam of ocean above and beyond the garden plants of Vailima – flamboyants, gardenias, avocados, mangoes, lemons and oranges, padanus, roses and cassias. Before the garden there had been a jungle track, up which the Stevensons' two packhorses, Donald and Edinburgh, had brought the first stores from Apia. Often the woods of Mount Vaea had been full of war drums. One of R.L.S.'s letters said, 'A man brought in a head in great glory; they washed the black [war] paint off, and behold! it was his brother. When I last heard he was sitting in his house, with the head upon his lap, and weeping.' Another letter told of warriors who 'brought in eleven heads, and to great horror and consternation . . . one proved to be a girl – a Maid of the village . . . It had been returned, wrapped in the most costly silk handkerchief, and with an apologetic embassy.'

Yet, in this room despite war drums, battle cries and maidens' heads, he had dictated stories of the cold, mist-bound north. Looking out at the drumless woods of Vaea, I thought: 'The early missionaries did at least bring peace, yet Stevenson was not against small 'hedge-wars'. They made the blood course; kept men on their toes. Men died, no doubt, but the race, purged and regenerated by battle, survived.

'Give me five minutes, Miki . . . to browse.'

I riffled the pages, stopping where I had made a pencil mark. Here, Stevenson was about to negotiate a truce between battling Samoans: 'I must ride barefoot . . . Twenty miles ride, ten of the miles in drenching rain, seven of them fasting in a morning chill, and six stricken hours political discussion by an interpreter; to say nothing of sleeping in a native house, at which many of our excellent literati would look askance of itself.' The energy of a semi-invalid. His wife Fanny said, 'Sometimes he looks like an old man, and then, at a moment's notice, he's a pretty brown boy.' And here was an ordinary day:

Wake at the first peep of day, come gradually to, and had a turn on the verandah before 5.55, at 6 breakfast; 6.10, to work . . . till 10.30; 11, luncheon. Make music furiously [on the flageolet] till about 2 . . . Work again till 4: fool from 4 to half-past, 4.30, bath; 5, dinner; smoke, chat on verandah, then hand of cards, and at last 8 come up to my room with a pint of beer and hard biscuit: turn in.

It was on the verandah that the end had come. Mrs Stevenson wrote:

My beloved son was suddenly called home last evening. At six o'clock he was well, hungry for dinner, and helping Fanny to make a Mayonnaise sauce; when suddenly he put both hands to his head and said, 'Oh, what a pain!' and then added, 'Do I look strange?' Fanny said no, not wishing to alarm him, and helped him into the hall, where she put him into the nearest easy chair. She called for us to come, but he was unconscious before I reached his side . . . At ten minutes past 8 p.m. all was over . . .

The police band had shambled away down the drive. Two gardeners in red-and-yellow lava-lavas were cutting back the creeper by the verandah. There was a great whistling of birds.

We brought a bed into the hall, and he was lifted on to it.

When all was over his boys gathered about him, and the chiefs of Tanugamanono (the nearest village) arrived with fine mats which they laid over the bed, bowing and saying, '*Talofa, Tusitala*'; and then, after kissing him and sitting a while in silence, they bowed again, and saying, '*Tofa, Tusitala*', and went out.

It was hot already. Miki nodded his snowy head towards the back of the house and poured me iced water in the head of state's kitchen, where R.L.S.'s cook, Talolo, had prepared Scottish food – stewed beef and potatoes, and soda scones – as well as baked bananas, and pineapple in claret. I took Miki's pale hand in both of mine and thanked him. 'Pleasant to have a visitor who knows the Tusitala,' the reedy voice said. 'Come again.'

I found Tolu and the others sprawling patiently under the trees, and we set off to climb the mountain in an atmosphere like wet gauze.

My notes at this point are disfigured by drops of sweat:

A hard climb. Mount Vaea stands 700 feet above Vailima, and we take the 'fast', straight-up track. How on earth did old Mrs Stevenson manage to follow Louis' coffin – borne by chiefs – to the top? If she could, I can. Underfoot, the track is muddy and covered with sodden leaves. Even Tolu, who has not seen Mount Vaea before but should be fit with farming and cricket, sweats heavily. 'The hill is very angry,' he says, meaning 'high'. It is all very well for the young – Fili, Amosa and Isaia hitch up their lava-lavas and disappear into the trees like woodcock. Their cries make the wood seem as if it's full of taunting *aitus*.

Manino and Emma keep with me. Manino's stomach is upset, but she insists on coming. I have given her Lomotil. She plods gamely upwards, giving me a warm smile now and then. Thirty minutes' steep, slippery climb. I feel crippled. My legs need to rest. Luckily there is a bench halfway up. Two young Samoans, running down, call in English a cheerful 'Good morning.' Up and up. And at last at the top. Unexpected Samoan music – a group of Samoan boys and girls are playing guitars under the trees. We sit and listen and cool off. Manino, smiling all the time, fans herself with a red and white handkerchief. The Lomotil seems to have done the trick. Isaia appropriates my binoculars. The crest of Mount Vaea is a wide, open space sloping towards the bay, hanging over Vailima. The tomb is white and rectangular, shaded by trees. R.L.S. lying in the earth here would only have to lift his head to see the ocean.

Fili's fingers run casually over the bronze lettering on the plaque: '1850 Robert Louis Stevenson 1894'. Amosa lightly polishes the raised letters of R.L.S.'s own *Requiem*:

> *Here he lies where he longed to be;*
> *Home is the sailor, home from the sea,*
> *And the hunter home from the hill.*

It is not love of Tusitala, of course. It is just a feeling they have . . .

On a second plaque a quotation in Samoan from 'Ruta I, 16–17'. When I look it up in English it reads:

And Ruth said, Entreat me not to leave thee, or to return from following after thee; for whither thou goest, I will go; and where thou lodgest, I will lodge; thy people shall be my people and thy God, my God: where thou diest, will I die, and there will I be buried: the Lord do so to me, and more also if aught but death part thee and me.

Beneath the words, a dying wreath of peonies. Red-bodied dragonflies dart like inquisitive spirits. The peace is exquisite. Manino begins to comb out her hair, letting it fall thick and black to her waist. Isaia is in a tree, his *aitu*'s cheek resting on a branch.

'See.' Tolu is pointing. Below us, through dark ancient trees a bright green lawn, the blue of Vailima's sunlit roof. East, rising land and forest; a mountaintop lost in cloud; the silver wriggle of a river. South, the ocean; and the glittering pond of the harbour, with three small ships at anchor within the white curve of surf. The faint sigh of waves on the reef.

An old man comes quietly out of the trees, grey and very grizzled, carrying a bush knife and a basket full of cut shrubs. To me, he says,

'The leaves I have make the patient be healed,' In clear English, holding up a leaf. To the view, he says, 'Such beautiful sights.'

He chats in Samoan with Tolu and Fili, turns again to me. 'Where – may I ask you – is your home situated? Oh! So near to home of the Tusitala. The same country! And you come all this way . . .' He waved a hand. 'These friends say you are a writer, sir.'

I smile and point to the almost empty hilltop we stand on. 'Do you think there's space for me here?'

'Oh, plenty. Certainly, space.' He smiles back, pointing down to Vailima. 'I live near the pastor's house in Vailima, sir. I have several books by Mr Robert Louis Stevenson in my house. Come and see.' He waves, drifting away.

It is hot. And silent. The singers have gone. Fili sleeps. Amosa sits cross-legged in the shade, slowly blinking enigmatic eyes, like a cat. Tolu stares at the sea. Manino pulls petals off a flower. Emma is combing Isaia's hair. For half an hour, except for a murmur or two, we are all silent. But it is getting *too* hot. 'Shall we go?' We begin the descent. Tolu, Manino, Emma and I descend sedately. Fili, Amosa and Isaia fly ahead as usual, and again the mountainside echoes like an aviary with their cries. In this damp heat I am glad to reach the falls in the valley where you cross over to the 'Road of Loving Hearts' the Samoans had built for Stevenson. He had admired these great forest trees. He heard the waterfall in that valley, the 'wonderful fine glen' at the bottom of the mountain. The house for him was 'a place for angels'.

I was leaving Samoa, old and new.

Had I only known the Tolu family for the inside of a week? We said our goodbyes near the Apia market. Tolu's smile was solemn when he shook hands. 'Thank you,' he said. Manino, blinking, said, '*Tofa*,' and Emma, 'Come next year.'

Taking her hand, I said, 'Try to be here then, Emma. Stay in Samoa and teach.'

To Amosa: '*Tofa*, wood demon.'

His green-brown slanting eyes smiled. '*Tofa*, Gavin.'

'Come next year,' Fili said.

It was difficult to get Isaia to leave the car. He had slept in it every night and now it was his, he thought, as much as mine. I led him out by the hand and brushed his tears away and kissed his forehead.

'*Tofa, aitu*.' I tapped his nose to make him smile. Then I ducked into the car and drove off, waving from the window without looking back. The flowers Ruta and Isaia had scattered on the dashboard were beginning to wilt by now, and I let them lie when I left the car at Aggie Grey's. I noticed something on the back seat. It was Amosa's bush lime. For a moment or two I sniffed its delicate perfume. Then I slipped it into my pocket as a souvenir.

'So travel doesn't always broaden the mind, eh?' Captain Tony Carter said. We were standing on the bridge wing of the China Navigation Company's container ship *Pacific Islander*, watching the receding shore of Western Samoa.

'In the case of some Samoans, it seems it may destroy it,' I said. The blue roofs of Vailima were visible on the left slope of Mount Vaea. I felt as if I had left something there I would have to go back for.

'And were those missionaries the first you'd ever met?'

'Almost,' I said. 'The first was a young Methodist in a sampan, halfway up the Chindwin River. In Burma. Quite remote. I was travelling illegally to the Chinese–Indian border to write about guerrilla war in the jungle there. No one was sure it existed.'

'And did it?'

'Oh, it existed all right. But thanks to that missionary I nearly missed it. You see, I was pretending to be a missionary myself – they were the only foreigners allowed up that way.'

I saw again the overloaded sampan and the great meandering, muddy river, and my chicken coop of a cabin on the hot metal deck. The sampan made slow progress. It went aground on every second sandbank, and we had to wait for the crew to pole us off. I hadn't actually told anyone I was a missionary, but I suppose the two Bibles I carried rather ostentatiously amounted to a disguise. I expected trouble as soon as I saw the white man in sarong and sandals on the bamboo jetty, waiting to come aboard and share the chicken coop. He had a stack of Bibles tied up with string. There was trouble, too. He took one look at me, my Bibles and my whisky bottle, and said he was going to denounce me to the local police. Interlopers like me should be made to suffer.

The Burmese police officers squatting outside the coop, tirelessly playing cards and smoking, were on their way to upriver posts; their specific object was to trap unauthorized foreigners like me. One call and I would have faced a Rangoon jail for . . . well, indefinitely.

'He took a righteous view, did he, this missionary bloke?' asked Tony Carter.

'Not as it turned out. You see, he'd got an idea I really was a missionary – a Seventh Day Adventist come to poach his Burmese converts. When I told him I was a journalist travelling *sub rosa*, he became as friendly as anything. Even forgave me my whisky.'

Carter laughed.

'His name was Edwards, and he came from Reading. I sometimes wonder what became of him.'

The *Pacific Islander* had left Apia for Pago–Pago and Papeete on the afternoon of my visit to Mount Vaea. There had been no problems. Tim Bridgeman in Hong Kong had telexed the company's permission for me to board her, subject to her master's agreement, and Tony Carter, I soon realized, was another of the China Navigation Company's friendly officers. There was a bonus, too: Steve Komorowski, the second officer, was an acquaintance from the *Hupeh* of two years before. I had told him to read Joseph Conrad: their names were similar.

Then there was Miss Yip, the radio officer.

Miss Yip Pui Fun was no relation at all to Angel Yip who had helped me to Shanghai. This Miss Yip was small, trim and wore her hair pulled back tautly over her ears – and she was afraid of men. Chris Macdonald, the mate, said with a wicked grin, 'She has fixed a very strong bolt on her door. She takes it with her from ship to ship. So if you're thinking . . .'

Miss Yip, I thought, was an appropriate person to meet at this stage of the voyage, if she had any puritanical affinity with Somerset Maugham's Mrs Davidson, the intolerant, hypocritical missionary's insufferable wife in the short story *Rain*. Maugham was a shrewd setter of scenes. American Samoa is famous for its rainfall. We were now within a very short distance of the tiny port of Pago-Pago (pronounced Pango-Pango), where Maugham's character, Sadie Thompson, the hooker from San Francisco, ran into the appalling Mr Davidson.

Mrs Davidson had 'served' in Hawaii, and the Samoan lava-lava scandalized her as 'a very indecent costume'. How, she demanded in high-pitched tones, could you expect people to be moral when they wore nothing but a strip of red cotton round their loins? 'In our islands,' she proclaimed proudly, 'we practically eradicated the lava-lava. And the inhabitants of these 49 islands will never be thoroughly Christianized till every boy of more than ten years is made to wear a pair of trousers.'

My first meeting with Miss Yip was not encouraging. To my polite 'Good evening' she returned no answer at all.

In no time we were at the entrance to Pago-Pago – a horseshoe with an extremely narrow southern opening on to a long curve of beach with, behind it, a soaring, spectacular ruff of mountain and forest.

'Tricky entrance,' I said to Tony Carter.

'If you want to see a really narrow gap in a reef, wait until Papeete.'

'You push the buoys apart there,' Chris Macdonald added.

This was nothing like little Apia. Through my binoculars I saw a big modern hotel, bungalows that belonged in Los Angeles, large American limousines, and a lot of baseball caps and jeans. A hefty white rich man's fishing launch, prickly with antennae, roared out of the harbour as we came up to the wharf, and cable cars moved dizzily between two peaks on either side of the harbour abyss. Evidently, Pago-Pago had changed a lot more since 1920 than Apia or Suva. 'No town,' Maugham wrote of it then. 'Merely a group of official buildings, a store or two . . .' Sadie Thompson had called it 'a poor imitation of a burg'. But the Second World War had come and gone since Maugham, and the harbour had passed through a stage of being a great naval and Marine Corps base. The base had gone too, but Pago-Pago, though materially impoverished by its loss, had never reverted to the damp, sleepy place Maugham saw.

'Samoans here,' said Captain Carter, 'refer to "The Main-land". Guess what that means to them?'

'Tell me.'

'America. Can you believe it?'

'Not easily.'

Pago-Pago had not forgotten Somerset Maugham. The big modern hotel I had seen was called the Rainmaker, and it had a Sadie Thompson Bar. I wanted to see if it was on the site of Maugham's hotel, so I took Miss Yip there. I thought she might be lonely in the locked cabin by herself.

'I like to come,' she said, rather to my surprise.

'Are you worried on the ship with so many men?' I asked her.

'Filipinos frighten me,' she said. 'But this ship is quite okay. Because the crewmen are very old. Only the laundryman is twenty-five; the rest are not below forty.' The over-forties were past it in her estimation. No wonder she felt safe with me.

In fact, the Sadie Thompson Bar was the height of propriety. Appropriately, it was full of cheerful American sailors from a visiting warship, as well-behaved as the Broadway chorus of *South Pacific*. No one sang 'There is Nothing Like a Dame', but a jukebox jingled. At the bar with a phoney Samoan thatched roof, Miss Yip accepted a fruit cocktail – passion fruit, mango, milk, soda, grenadine. I kept her company with a *mai tai*: hefty jolts of three different rums mixed with fruit juice in a glass like a birdbath. Around us sailors called high-spiritedly for more Budweiser. 'Have a Happy Day' a bar sign said. Outside the plate-glass windows the rain poured down. 51

Old Maugham would have liked that. As for Miss Yip Pui Fun, she looked calmly around her, smiled, and accepted a second fruit cocktail. I liked her. Apart from anything else, she did somehow remind me of Angel Yip. When Pui Fun offered me a sweet I felt as if I had been awarded a good conduct medal.

Iniquity, according to the *Pacific Islander*'s good-natured third officer, Graham Harris, was to be found at a dive called the Pago Bar. 'A cross between the Butterfly Bar in the Bangkok docks and a flophouse in Singapore's Bugis Street of, well, twenty years ago,' he promised. 'Good chance of a punch-up to boot. The Korean trawlermen go there, mostly,' he said. 'They spend three months at sea non-stop, then come back here with all that stinking fish. You can imagine what *they* get up to.'

'But not you, of course,' Chris Macdonald said sarcastically.

'I'm getting married in six months. You can have those Samoan hags. I'd rather screw a tin of corned beef.'

'I believe you would an' all.'

The Korean trawlers lay all around; a fleet of battered rust-buckets, built for nothing but very rough work. Larger, more modern vessels were visible alongside the Star-Kist fish canning factory across the harbour. Several of the trawlers were strung about with lines on which diminutive Oriental underwear hung out like bunting. A Korean in a singlet and shorts was trying to manhandle a squealing pig up the gangway of No. 73 – the *Kwang Myong*. When darkness fell, the lights of the fish cannery shone across the water sharp and bright. It worked all through the night to keep American Samoa running.

'No beer taken outside' a sign said when we pushed through the door of the Pago Bar and into the fog of heat and smoke beyond. Koreans were thick on the ground by the time of night Chris, Graham, Steve and I got there, leaving Tony Carter on board singing to himself over a beer. A mirrored globe over a postage-stamp-sized dance floor scattered fragments of light over the tatters of leftover Christmas decorations on the ceiling. In the gloom I saw big male Samoan shapes in dark glasses, bearded and drunk, and women with bottoms like upholstered railway buffers. Most of the Koreans had long hair, and came in two sorts: James Bond's Oddjobs, with the look of killers who had volunteered for special homicide duty; or jolly Oriental dolls, red-faced with beer and only wanting a good time. Perhaps the Samoan hostesses were too big for some of them – they might have feared being crushed to death – because a few preferred to dance with each other. Soon, unbelievably, the atmosphere thickened even more. Vast dancing Samoan shapes wallowed through it like hippos in a mudhole. Beer came, was drunk, was reordered. I saw Komorowski swaying about with a woman as old as Boadicea's aunt. 'Oh, darling, to me be tree-ooo . . .' a pretty girl was singing on the tiny dais with a ragged trio of guitarists behind her. In the murk a bottle smashed on the floor and there was a sudden swirl of male figures beyond the bandstand. An elderly American sat down in Komorowski's place.

'They don't have to have it so loud,' he bawled into the gloom. 'Jeesus Christ!' He had a shining bald dome, and W. C. Fields' nose so pitted by heavy drinking that mice might have nibbled at it. 'They've no savvy. That's it,' he declared mournfully. 'No comprehenso.' He held up a fist and shook it at me. 'Don't say I said it.' 'I won't,' I promised.

Komorowski jigged by again, held fast this time in the arms of Whistler's granny in black-face. Even in this dungeon-like obscurity, the sweat gleamed on his brow like quicksilver. On my other side, a long-haired Korean – a jolly type, not a volunteer killer – was trying to entice Graham on to the dance floor: '*Tak-shee, tak-shee,*' he was imploring – or that's what it sounded like. Graham looked at me, making signs like a man drowning.

The Korean muttered again, '*Tak-shee, tak-shee.*'

I said, 'Have a little dance with him, Graham.'

'Go on, Graham,' Chris said, encouragingly.

'I'm getting married in six months, for God's sake.' But the Korean was speaking urgently now. '*Tak-shee, tak-shee – tak-shee!*'

'Get a move on, Graham, or he may turn nasty. He's been at sea three months, remember.'

'Here – put this whisky down for courage.'

Graham took the drink, but his face still wore an expression of desperation. 'You're just a couple of bloody sadists, throwing a young boy like me, that's about to be married, into the arms –'

'*Tak-shee, tak-shee! Bok!*'

54   'Graham!'

'Oh, blimey. All right. The things I do . . .'

He and the Korean dived together into the struggling mass, and the music – a Pacific version of 'Embraceable You' now – closed over them like animated treacle.

The old American said, 'No savvy, as far as the eye can see. Take a drink?'

I thanked him: 'A Scotch, please.'

A double came. The American was a drilling expert, he said; he drilled for anything – water, oil, gold – you name it.

Graham waltzed uneasily by, holding the smiling Korean almost daintily at arm's length. They might have been dancing ring-a-ring-o'-roses in slow motion.

The American said, 'Jee-sus Christ. You don't have to sleep alone in this place.' A smiling woman like Babar the Elephant came up to our table. 'Nice, but no comprehenso,' the American said, waving her away. 'No savvy. That's their trouble. But don't say I said so.' He ordered six more beers for the three of us.

'How old am I?' he demanded when they came.

'Sixty-two,' I said.

'Thanks very much.' He was gratified. 'I'm seventy-five. I'll buy you a drink.'

'A large Scotch,' I said.

Time passed.

Graham Harris's sweaty face went by yet again. By now his shirt clung to his back as if he'd been out in a rain storm. The Korean's left hand sat on his shoulder like a tarantula.

'Yoo-hoo!' somebody yelled at him. Perhaps it was Chris – 55 or me. Almost immediately, as if summoned by a war cry, two Koreans were standing in front of me, bowing their heads up and down like birds drinking.

'That's a kow-tow,' the American said. 'They're kow-towing you. It's the custom. *These* guys have plenty of savvy. Better be polite and give 'em a kow-tow back.'

But the kow-tow didn't save me. It turned into something between a Highland reel and a galloping version of Auld Lang Syne as the three of us bumped and crashed around the dance floor like dodgem cars at a fairground. I was luckier than Graham. The music soon changed to rock 'n' roll. The Samoans went wild, and the Koreans scuttled off the floor like terrified mice at an elephant round-up.

'No punch-ups?' Tony Carter said next day. 'That's odd. I expect you'd have liked a punch-up. You should have been with us New Year's Eve in Nuku'alofa with the Tongans. We had a good 'un there. The radio officer had to get back to the ship by walking along the top of a reef up to his waist in water!'

Pago-Pago had a sort of village green now and some attractive colonial-style wooden houses.

The tiny, dismal hotel in which poor Sadie Thompson had been bullied and then raped by Mr Davidson had actually existed – 'a frame house of two storeys, with broad verandahs on both floors and a roof of corrugated iron . . . On the ground floor, the owner (a half-caste named Horn) had a store where he sold canned goods and cottons.' I found a 'Sadie Thompson's Mart' in what was said to be the same building. It was a two-storey wooden structure, at any rate. I bought some plum-coloured cotton cloth there, half listening for some echo of Sadie's famous cry of contempt – 'You men! You filthy, dirty pigs! You're all the same, all of you. Pigs! Pigs!' And I took a turn down the long sweep of beach where kind Dr Macphail had seen, lying half in the water and half out, a dreadful object, Davidson's body . . . 'the throat cut from ear to ear, and in the right hand still the razor with which the deed was done'.

There was no one here now. Only the smell of fish from the canning factory, and dark clouds gathering overhead. As I reached the asphalted road to walk back to the ship, it began to rain.

READ MORE IN PENGUIN

For complete information about books available from Penguin and how to order them, please write to us at the appropriate address below. Please note that for copyright reasons the selection of books varies from country to country.

IN THE UNITED KINGDOM: Please write to *Dept. EP, Penguin Books Ltd, Bath Road, Harmondsworth, Middlesex UB7 0DA*.

IN THE UNITED STATES: Please write to *Consumer Sales, Penguin USA, P.O. Box 999, Dept. 17109, Bergenfield, New Jersey 07621-0120*. VISA and MasterCard holders call 1-800-253-6476 to order Penguin titles.

IN CANADA: Please write to *Penguin Books Canada Ltd, 10 Alcorn Avenue, Suite 300, Toronto, Ontario M4V 3B2*.

IN AUSTRALIA: Please write to *Penguin Books Australia Ltd, P.O. Box 257, Ringwood, Victoria 3134*.

IN NEW ZEALAND: Please write to *Penguin Books (NZ) Ltd, Private Bag 102902, North Shore Mail Centre, Auckland 10*.

IN INDIA: Please write to *Penguin Books India Pvt Ltd, 706 Eros Apartments, 56 Nehru Place, New Delhi 110 019*.

IN THE NETHERLANDS: Please write to *Penguin Books Netherlands bv, Postbus 3507, NL-1001 AH Amsterdam*.

IN GERMANY: Please write to *Penguin Books Deutschland GmbH, Metzlerstrasse 26, 60594 Frankfurt am Main*.

IN SPAIN: Please write to *Penguin Books S. A., Bravo Murillo 19, 1° B, 28015 Madrid*.

IN ITALY: Please write to *Penguin Italia s.r.l., Via Felice Casati 20, I-20124 Milano*.

IN FRANCE: Please write to *Penguin France S. A., 17 rue Lejeune, F-31000 Toulouse*.

IN JAPAN: Please write to *Penguin Books Japan, Ishikiribashi Building, 2-5-4, Suido, Bunkyo-ku, Tokyo 112*.

IN GREECE: Please write to *Penguin Hellas Ltd, Dimocritou 3, GR-106 71 Athens*.

IN SOUTH AFRICA: Please write to *Longman Penguin Southern Africa (Pty) Ltd, Private Bag X08, Bertsham 2013*.